# Introducing Continents

# Australia

Anita Ganeri

Raintree

Raintree is an imprint of Capstone Global Library Limited, a company incorporated in England and Wales having its registered office at 7 Pilgrim Street, London, EC4V 6LB – Registered company number: 6695582

www.raintreepublishers.co.uk
myorders@raintreepublishers.co.uk

Text © Capstone Global Library Limited 2014
First published in hardback in 2014
Paperback edition first published in 2015
The moral rights of the proprietor have been asserted.

Edited by Dan Nunn, Rebecca Rissman, Sian Smith, and Helen Cox Cannons
Designed by Philippa Jenkins
Original illustrations © Capstone Global Library Ltd 2014
Picture research by Liz Alexander and Tristan Leverett
Production by Vicki Fitzgerald
Originated by Capstone Global Library Ltd
Printed and bound in China by Leo Paper Products Ltd

ISBN 978 1 406 26296 4 (hardback)
17 16 15 14 13
10 9 8 7 6 5 4 3 2 1

ISBN 978 1 406 26305 3 (paperback)
18 17 16 15 14
10 9 8 7 6 5 4 3 2 1

**British Library Cataloguing in Publication Data**
Ganeri, Anita
Introducing Australia. – (Introducing continents)
A full catalogue record for this book is available from the British Library.

**Acknowledgements**
We would like to thank the following for permission to reproduce photographs: Alamy pp. 13 (© Steffan Hill), 18 (© Bill Bachman), 21 (© Paul Kingsley); Corbis pp.23 (© Marianna Massey), 27 (© Kit Kittle); Getty Images pp. 8 (Ted Mead/Photolibrary), 9 (Pawel Toczynski/Photolibrary), 10 (Jason Edwards /National Geographic), 12 (Photo By Martin Cohen Wild About Australia/Lonely Planet Images), 20 (Sharon Smith/ AFP). 22 (Quinn Rooney), 25 (Gallo Images/ Danita Delimont); naturepl.com pp. 14 (© Ingo Arndt), 15 (© Doug Perrine); Shutterstock pp. 6 (© Susan Harris), 11 (© Alberto Loyo), 16 (© Szekeres Szabolcs), 17 (© Ashley Whitworth), 19 bottom (© Alexander Hoffmann), 26 (© Phillip Minnis); SuperStock pp. 7 (age footstock), 19 top.

Cover photographs of an outback road in Northern Territory, Australia and a shaded relief map of Australia reproduced with permission of Shutterstock (© Ralph Loesche, © AridOcean); image of three Aborigines playing musical instruments reproduced with permission of SuperStock (© Robert Harding Picture Library).

Every effort has been made to contact copyright holders of material reproduced in this book. Any omissions will be rectified in subsequent printings if notice is given to the publisher.

**Disclaimer**
All the internet addresses (URLs) given in this book were valid at the time of going to press. However, due to the dynamic nature of the internet, some addresses may have changed, or sites may have changed or ceased to exist since publication. While the author and publisher regret any inconvenience this may cause readers, no responsibility for any such changes can be accepted by either the author or the publisher.

# Contents

Some words are shown in bold, **like this**. You can find out what they mean by looking in the glossary.

# About Australia

A **continent** is a huge area of land. There are seven continents on Earth. This book is about the continent of Australia. Australia is the world's smallest continent.

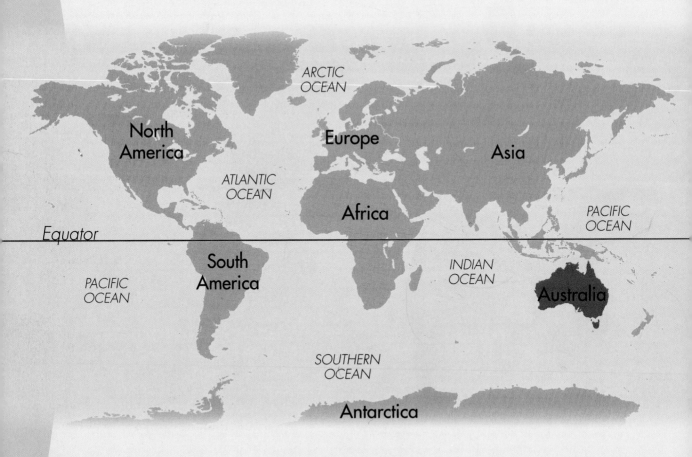

ARCTIC OCEAN

North America

Europe

Asia

ATLANTIC OCEAN

Africa

PACIFIC OCEAN

Equator

PACIFIC OCEAN

South America

INDIAN OCEAN

Australia

SOUTHERN OCEAN

Antarctica

Australia is a huge island. It is surrounded by the Indian Ocean and the Pacific Ocean. Australia also includes the island of Tasmania to the south.

| Australia fact file | |
| --- | --- |
| Area | 7,713,364 square kilometres (2,966,136 square miles) |
| Population | 22 million |
| Number of countries | 1 |
| Highest mountain | Mount Kosciuszko at 2,229 metres (7,313 feet) |
| Longest river | Murray-Darling at 3,824 kilometres (2,376 miles) |

# Famous places

There are many famous places in Australia. Some are modern. The Sydney Opera House opened in 1973. It has become one of the most famous buildings in the world. Its roof looks like a ship's sails.

The Sydney Opera House stands in Sydney Harbour.

Uluru stands 335 metres (1,100 feet) high. It used to be called Ayers Rock.

Some famous places are very old. Uluru is a giant hill of red rock in central Australia. It is a **sacred** place for the **Aboriginal** people. It has many caves and ancient rock paintings.

# Geography

Huge, dry **deserts** cover large parts of western and central Australia. The biggest is the Great Victoria Desert. It is famous for its red **sand dunes**.

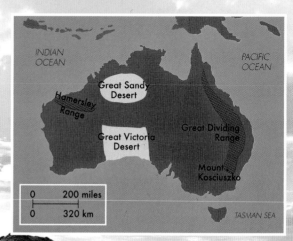

INDIAN OCEAN

PACIFIC OCEAN

Great Sandy Desert

Hamersley Range

Great Victoria Desert

Great Dividing Range

Mount Kosciuszko

| 0 | 200 miles |
| 0 | 320 km |

TASMAN SEA

The Great Victoria Desert has sand dunes, pebbly plains, and salt lakes.

Mount Kosciuszko is in the Snowy Mountains in southeast Australia.

A long line of mountains runs down the eastern side of Australia. It is called the Great Dividing Range. To the south is the highest mountain in Australia – Mount Kosciuszko. It is 2,229 metres (7,313 feet) tall.

The Murray and Darling rivers join up to make the Murray-Darling River. It is the longest river in Australia. It flows for 3,824 kilometres (2,376 miles) from the Great Dividing Range into the sea.

The land around the Murray-Darling River is good for farming.

Lake Eyre looks almost empty here. It fills up again after heavy rains.

Lake Eyre is the biggest lake in Australia. It is filled with **saltwater**, but often dries out in the heat. The lake has only been full of water three times in the last 100 years.

# Weather

Most of Australia has hot, dry weather. When it is very dry, there is a risk of Bushfires breaking out. The far north and north east have warm weather with lots of rain.

Bushfires spread very quickly if the ground is dry.

In Australia, Christmas is in the summer time. Some Australians spend Christmas on the beach.

Australia is in the Southern Hemisphere. It has opposite seasons to the Northern Hemisphere. Winter lasts from June to August. Summer lasts from December to February.

# Animals

Australia's most famous animals are **marsupials**, such as koalas and kangaroos. These are animals that carry their babies in pouches. Many unusual birds also live in Australia, such as kookaburras and emus.

A kangaroo carries its baby, or joey, in its pouch.

Thousands of multi-coloured fish swim on the Great Barrier Reef.

The Great Barrier Reef stretches along the northeast coast of Australia. It is the biggest **coral reef** on Earth. It is home to an astonishing number of animals. They include around 1,500 types of fish.

# Plants

Many unusual plants grow in Australia. Eucalyptus trees, sometimes called gum trees, grow all over the **continent**. Their leaves make a strong-smelling oil. Eucalyptus leaves are the favourite food of koalas.

Koalas eat so many eucalyptus leaves that they smell of eucalyptus.

The seeds of the Sturt's desert pea can sprout very quickly after a shower of rain.

The Sturt's desert pea is a plant that grows in the **desert**. It has bunches of bright-red and black flowers. Its seeds lie in the hot ground. They grow very quickly as soon as it rains.

# Natural resources

Australia has many **natural resources**. About two-thirds of the land is used for farming. In the dry **outback**, farmers keep sheep on enormous farms. The sheep are mainly kept for their wool.

These merino sheep are raised for their soft, fine wool.

This digger is working on an opal mine in Australia.

Many metals, such as gold and iron **ore**, are **mined** in Australia. There are also huge diamond mines. Most of the world's **opals** come from Australia. The **continent** is also rich in oil, gas, and coal.

polished opal

# People

About 22 million people live in Australia. Most people are **descended from** Europeans who settled in Australia. Other people have come from Asian countries, such as China and Vietnam.

These Australian schoolchildren come from many different backgrounds.

These Aboriginal children are dressed in traditional costume for a dance.

The **Aboriginals** were the first people to live in Australia. They came from South East Asia around 40,000 years ago. They used to move from place to place, but now many live in cities and towns.

# Sport and culture

Sport is very popular in Australia. Many Australians play or watch cricket, rugby, and Australian rules football. Australian rules football is played on a oval-shaped field. It is like a cross between rugby and football.

These men are playing Australian rules football in Melbourne.

This Aboriginal artist is creating a dot painting.

The **Aboriginal** people have their own art and music which is thousands of years old. They paint pictures using dots of different colours. The paintings usually show animals or pictures from Aboriginal stories.

# Countries

There is just one country in the **continent** of Australia and that is Australia! Australia is divided into six **states** and two **territories**. The largest Australian state is Western Australia.

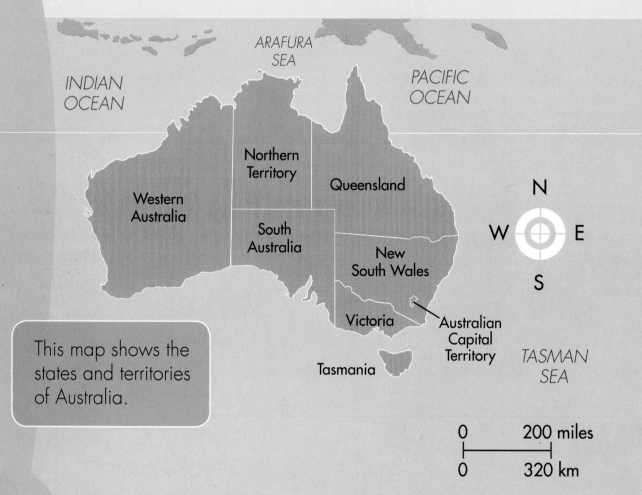

This map shows the states and territories of Australia.

This is one of the islands that make up Fiji in the South Pacific Ocean.

Australia is part of a much bigger region, called Oceania. Oceania also includes New Zealand, Papua New Guinea, and thousands of islands in the South Pacific Ocean.

# Cities and countryside

There are many big, modern cities in Australia. Canberra is the capital of Australia. It is home to the Australian **parliament**. Sydney is the biggest city. It is famous for its harbour and harbour bridge.

The famous harbour bridge in Sydney is made from steel.

A "flying doctor" arrives at the scene of a car accident.

People in the **outback** often live far away from cities and towns. If people fall ill or have an accident, a "flying doctor" goes out to visit them in a plane. Some children living in the outback have to do their lessons by radio or on the computer.

# Fun facts

- Australia is a huge island. It is also a **continent** and a country.

- Eight of the world's ten most deadly snakes live in Australia.

- In Australia, there are about three sheep for every one person.

- More than three-quarters of Australians live in towns and cities.

# Quiz

1. What is the capital of Australia?

2. Who were the first people to live in Australia?

3. Does Australia lie above or below the equator?

4. Name two types of **marsupials**.

4. Kangaroos and koalas

3. Below

2. Aboriginals

1. Canberra

# Glossary

**Aboriginal** first people to live in Australia

**continent** one of seven huge areas of land on Earth

**coral reefs** rocky structures built by tiny sea creatures

**descended from** related to someone long ago

**desert** hot, dry place that has very little rain

**marsupials** animals that carry their young in pouches

**mined** dug up from under the ground

**natural resources** natural materials that we use, such as wood, coal, oil, and rock

**opal** a type of precious stone

**ore** rock that contains metals

**outback** dry land in the middle of Australia

**parliament** group of people that makes a country's laws

**sacred** special or holy

**saltwater** water that is salty, like the sea

**sand dunes** huge piles of sand in the desert

**states** areas of Australia that make their own laws

**territories** areas of Australia with their own laws

# Find out more

## Books

*Australia* (Exploring Continents), Jane Bingham (Heinemann Library, 2008)

*Horrible Geography of the World*, Anita Ganeri (Scholastic, 2010)

*Oxford First Atlas* (OUP, 2010)

## Websites to visit

**kids.discovery.com/tell-me/people-and-places/ our-7-continents**
Various games, puzzles, and activities about the seven continents can be found on this website.

**kids.nationalgeographic.com/kids/games/ geographygames/copycat**
This fun game helps you to find the continents on a map of the world.

**www.worldatlas.com**
This site has lots of maps, facts, and figures about continents.

# Index